# MOUNTAIN BIKING

## by Alicia and Rusty Schoenherr

*Content Adviser: J.J. Jameson, Director,*
*Dirt Camp, Redding, Connecticut*

Published in the United States of America by The Child's World®
PO Box 326 • Chanhassen, MN 55317-0326 • 800-599-READ • www.childsworld.com

## Acknowledgments

The Child's World®: Mary Berendes, Publishing Director

Editorial Directions, Inc.: E. Russell Primm, Editorial Director; Melissa McDaniel, Line Editor; Matt Messbarger, Project Editor and Editorial Assistant; Susan Hindman, Copy Editor; Susan Ashley, Proofreader; Terry Johnson, Olivia Nellums, Katharine Trickle, and Julie Zaveloff, Fact Checkers; Tim Griffin/IndexServ, Indexer; James Buckley Jr. and James Gigliotti, Photo Researchers and Selectors

Editorial and photo research services provided by Shoreline Publishing Group LLC, Santa Barbara, California

The Design Lab: Kathleen Petelinsek, Art Direction and Design; Kari Thornborough, Art Production

## Photos

Cover: Photodisc/Punchstock; Ales Fevzer/Corbis: 7, 8, 14, 21, 24; Bettmann/Corbis: 6; Charlie Samuels/Corbis: 17; Chase Jarvis/Corbis: 19; Corbis: 5, 20; David Stoecklein/Corbis: 23; Duomo/Corbis: 27; Getty Images: 11, 12, 13, 28; Mark Hanauer/Corbis: 15; Reuters New Media Inc./Corbis: 25, 26.

## Library of Congress Cataloging-in-Publication Data

Schoenherr, Alicia.
   Mountain biking / by Alicia and Rusty Schoenherr.
      v. cm. — (Kids' guides)
   Includes bibliographical references and index.
   Contents: The klunkers—Gearing up to ride—Mountain biking in action—Superstars of the mountains.
      ISBN 1-59296-209-2 (library bound : alk. paper) 1. All terrain cycling—Juvenile literature.
[1. All terrain cycling.] I. Schoenherr, Alicia. II. Title. III. Series.
   GV1056.S36 2005
   796.63—dc22                                        2003027371

# CONTENTS

# FROM STREET TO TRAIL

## Most of you have probably ridden a

bike on the sidewalk, down a street, or in a park. But what about riding on the grass, up a dirt hill, or down a snow-covered mountain? The sport of mountain biking combines riding a bike with great outdoor adventure. It doesn't always involve a real mountain, but it usually involves riding where there's no pavement.

People have been riding bicycles for more than 150 years. Although mountain biking is a fairly new sport, there were always some people who rode bikes off-road. The development of special bikes and equipment for mountain biking simply made blazing trails safer and easier. Adventure-loving cyclists now ride just about anywhere that cars can't go. Mountain bikers will ride in the mud, snow, and sand, over steep cliffs and rocks, and even up and down stairs.

Professional mountain bikers practice for many hours a day and have top-quality bikes and gear. But all you really need is a helmet, a bike with fat tires, and an unpaved area to ride. Mountain biking can mean a nice, calm ride though the woods, or it can mean barreling down a ski slope. Anyone who can ride a bike on pavement can learn to mountain bike. Just expect to get dirty and have fun.

Whatever the terrain, mountain biking is a blast.

# CHAPTER one

# THE KLUNKERS

## The first bikes looked a lot like those

we have now, except they had no pedals or handlebars and they were made of wood, including the wheels. In 1817, a bike with handlebars was invented, but it still had no pedals. Instead, it was moved by foot power (sort of like Fred Flintstone's car). By 1865, the "bone shaker" was made. This one had pedals. Bouncing over the rough roads of the time really shook up the rider. Then, around 1870, people started building high-wheel bikes, which had a large front tire and a tiny back tire, both made of solid rubber. A high-wheel bike was fine until you had to stop quickly. Then the rider usually took a **header** and landed upside down in the street.

Would you like to have gone off-road with one of these? Didn't think so!

Luckily, by the 1880s metal bikes with chains (and the previously mentioned rubber tires) became popular. They were much more comfortable to ride than earlier bikes. These metal bikes were the original mountain bikes. Because few roads were paved at that time,

Today's custom bikes have come a long way from the high-wheelers.

*everything* was off-road. In the 1930s, the first fat-tire bikes were built. Narrow tires, such as those found on racing bikes, improve speed over smooth surfaces. Fat tires, on the other hand, offer greater stability and durability on bumpy surfaces.

In the 1970s, a group of men in Cupertino, California, decided to alter their bikes to make them better for off-road biking. These friends, who called themselves the Morrow Dirt Club, changed biking forever. They took their regular old bikes

The vision of the mountain-bike pioneers led to off-road racing.

and added equipment to them so they could ride in the mountains of California. The men added fatter tires, motorcycle handlebars, and gears made for racing bikes. In 1974, they rode their **klunkers** in a race. The people watching couldn't believe what they saw. The men from the Morrow Dirt Club had made single-speed cruisers and flat-road bikes into five- and ten-speed mountain bikes. Adding the gears meant that the men could ride up the same trails that they then barreled down.

One of the men at the race was Gary Fisher, a bike racer. He saw these riders and their fat balloon tires and never forgot them. He started modifying bikes and racing them with his friends. In 1979, Fisher and his friend Charlie Kelly started a company called MountainBikes, which was the first use of this term. In its first year, the company made and sold more than 100 bikes. These were the first real commercial mountain bikes.

Mountain bikes today don't look much like the original klunkers. They still have two wheels, pedals, gears, and handle-bars. But new technology has created endless possibilities for such bikes. Fat tires are now routine on mountain bikes. Pedals are either flat or have **toe-clips.** Some riders have cleats on the bottom of their shoes that attach to the pedals. Many mountain bikes now have three different chain ring **sprockets** in front and up to nine gears in the back, which gives riders up to 27 possible speeds. Handlebars turn in, out, up, or down, depending on what each rider likes. The introduction of **shocks** on the frame and gel or padded seats has helped make for a more comfortable ride.

## SAFE TRAIL RIDING

As more people look to the outdoors for action sports fun, safety becomes ever more important. When riding on a trail, you might come across other bikers, runners, hikers, or even horses. Following these "Rules of the Trail" from the International Mountain Bicycling Association should help everyone have a safe time:

- Ride only on open trails. Don't ride on trails that are closed or where bicycling is not allowed.
- Leave no trace. Don't ride off the trail and don't litter.
- Control your bicycle. Obey speed limits and be aware of who or what might be around a turn.
- Always yield the trail. Bikers should let others on the trail know they're coming with a friendly whistle or a shout. No one wants to be run down by an out-of-control biker! Be prepared to slow down or even stop around people or animals.
- Never scare animals (or people!). Take extra care around horses and follow directions from the horseback riders.
- Plan ahead. Keep your bike in good condition, be prepared for a change in weather, and carry all the supplies you might need on a ride.

In the past few years, mountain biking has become more popular than road biking. When grown-ups mountain bike, they feel like kids, and when kids mountain bike, they can ride in the mud—on purpose! Those friends in California had the right idea. Grab a bike, your helmet, and a bunch of friends, and head out for adventure.

# GEARING UP TO RIDE

## The gear needed to have fun mountain

biking is simple. You need a bike and a helmet—that's about it!

For more comfort and safety, you can add jerseys, gloves, biking

shorts, knee and shin guards, or even rearview mirrors.

Choosing the right mountain bike is the first step in your

adventure on the trails. A good bike shop will help you pick a

bike that is the right size for you. Here are some details about

the parts of your bike:

Grab a bike
and helmet, and
you're ready to
get started!

It's important to decide on the right bike—handlebars and all.

## Handlebars

The original mountain bike handlebars were straight. Today, most bikes have bars that sweep back and rise up from the center. Check out the many styles available and see what's comfortable for you.

## Gears

Most mountain bikes for younger riders now have five or six gears in the back and one in the front. This number of gears allows beginning riders to shift easily. To shift, you click the shifter on the handlebar with your left or right hand. Lower gears help you gain speed and power; higher gears make it easier to pedal and help when climbing. As mentioned previously, top-level mountain bikes can have up to 27 gears, or speeds.

A bike's pedals, frame, and gears all are important considerations.

## Pedals

There are two types of pedals: foot on top and clipless. The first allows you to use any shoe. It is best to wear shoes that cover you whole foot and that have sticky soles. You can also get toe clips. Clipless pedals let you attach your feet to the pedals without using toe clips. To do this, you have to wear special cycling shoes that have a cleat on the bottom that "clicks" right to the pedal. To release the shoe from the pedal, you gently twist your foot. Though clipless pedals make for more efficient pedaling, for most young riders, foot on top pedals are better.

Don't forget the feet—choose the pedals and the shoes that are right for you.

## Shocks

Shocks are spring-loaded devices that compress slightly when you go over bumps, making the ride smoother. At first, mountain bikes had shocks only on the front wheels. Shocks on the rear wheels are a newer invention. They give riders more confidence and control and are included on most bikes for young riders.

With the right equipment, you're ready for some serious biking!

## Frame

Mountain bikes are smaller and shorter than racing bikes. They are also sturdier, so they can absorb the bouncing of the trail. Bikes today are made of steel, aluminum, carbon fiber, titanium, or a combination of these. Steel provides the smoothest ride. Aluminum is light and stiff. Titanium and carbon fiber are both durable and light, but they are also the most expensive. For kids, the least expensive material, steel, is the most widely used.

## HELMET HEAD

You may not like how you look in a helmet, but you would look a lot worse if you took a header without one. Though a helmet can be hot and heavy, it should be the first thing you put on for a ride. Making sure your helmet fits right is the first step to comfort and, more importantly, safety. Here are some important helmet tips:

- Make sure the helmet has a safety sticker approving it for bicycle use (look for the letters CPSC, ASTM, or Snell).
- The helmet should be snug on your head, covering the area from your forehead in the front to the base of your skull in the back.
- You should be able to fit one finger between your chin and the strap. If you can put more than one finger in that space, you need to tighten the strap.
- The helmet should not be able to move very much from side to side. If it does, tighten the straps on the sides.
- If the helmet can tilt down to your eyebrows, it is too loose. Tighten the straps on the sides.
- Put your helmet on and keep it on throughout the entire ride.

Mountain bikes come in any color you can imagine, often with designs or stripes. And many have cool names such as Rockhopper or Stumpjumper.

### Other Gear

There are other pieces of gear that can make your ride more comfortable. Jerseys both absorb sweat and protect your skin against scratches and scrapes. Soft leather gloves with padding on the palm add comfort to the ride. Gloves come in fingerless or full-finger styles. Some have mesh backing to help keep your hands cool.

Bike shorts have padded inserts on the seat that protect against bumps on the trail. Probably the best gear you can choose (besides a helmet, of course; see sidebar on page 16) are guards. Shin, knee, elbow, rib, and shoulder guards act as armor to protect your body. No matter how great a rider you are, you'll probably fall, especially while you're learning. Why not get a little help with some padding?

Even the most experienced rider knows the value of protective gear.

# MOUNTAIN BIKING IN ACTION

## As mountain biking has become more

and more popular, the number of places to ride has also grown. After testing a bike on a flat surface, you are ready to go. When heading out with your mountain bike, first make sure mountain biking is allowed in the area you want to go. Most places will have signs saying who can be on the trail, such as only walkers or no horses. Bikes are welcome on most trails. This is usually because the bikers who came before you were courteous and respectful toward others and the trail. Plan on being a courteous rider as well when you go!

Single track and double track trails are the most popular types of mountain biking trails. A single track is a trail so narrow that riders can only ride in single-file, one in front of the other. These tracks are about as wide as the handlebars of a bike and often wind through trees or brush. Bikers love these trails because they never know what might come next. Single track is not for a first-time rider. Save these trails for when you are really used to your bike and are not afraid to take a chance.

A double track trail is wide enough for two riders side-by-side and is usually good for beginning riders. Two people can ride together and see the whole trail. Many double tracks are fire roads or logging trails. They go up into the hills and moun-

Single-biker trails keep you close to Mother Nature.

tains and are steep on the downhill. But compared to single

track, they give you a little more room to spread out on the trail

and look for wildlife.

Sometimes the mountain in mountain-bike riding is covered with snow.

A new trend in mountain biking involves riding in ski areas when they're not covered in snow. You can ride up the slopes and then come down fast. Some ski areas will actually take you and your bike up the chairlift and let you off at the top. The ski runs provide a perfect ride down the mountain. Some have double tracks down the face of the mountain, while others include single tracks through the trees. Some experienced riders even bike these trails in the winter when the ground is covered with snow and ice!

Once you have mastered mountain bike skills, consider entering a race. There are two main types of mountain bike races: cross-country and downhill. In a cross-country race, all the riders start out together and the first one across the line wins. There are many obstacles on the way to the finish line, however. A typical race involves a fast, flat start leading to a single track through trees and sometimes through streams and over rocks. Then riders race up a steep hill and back down another long, steep hill to the finish.

And they're off! These riders begin a race in Durango, Colorado.

## TRAIL CARE

Here's a great job: you travel the country with your bike, riding old trails and checking out spots for new ones. The International Mountain Bicycling Association and Subaru of America sponsor the Trail Care Crew. This group of men and women is responsible for many trails in the United States, and some in Europe and Canada.

Since 1997, the crew has been working to improve the quality and safety of trails for mountain bikers. In 2003 alone, they assisted on projects in California, Florida, and 10 states in between. The crew works with local bikers to clean up old trails and keep them safe. They meet with government officials to get new trails made. Many volunteers make the work go much faster. Chances are that any trail you try has been ridden first by one of the Trail Care Crew.

A cross-country race can be anywhere from 1 mile (1.7 kilometers) to 100 miles (169 km) long, with lots of uphills along the way. Some races even last 24 hours! The racers don't always know the course, so they have to be able to anticipate what is coming and adjust their riding to the trail. Even if you have raced a trail before, rain can turn the trail to mud, rocks can slide, or a tree may be over the road. Cross-country racers have to think fast and ride even faster.

A downhill race is different because the riders start out one at a time and race the clock. Downhill riders wear much more gear to protect themselves, including goggles, a full-face helmet, and shoulder, shin, and knee guards. Before the race, they are allowed to inspect the course to check out the obstacles they will face. There may be quick turns, jumps, steep curves, and perhaps even a set of stairs! You never know. Downhill racers can reach speeds up to 60 miles (97 km) per hour. The rider with the fastest time wins.

The National Off-Road Bicycle Association organizes races for all ages and levels. Bike shops are often the best source of information on races. They know where the races are and who can ride. In some areas, bike clubs organize races and festivals. Once you decide you want to race, you will have no trouble finding somewhere to do it.

Who knows? With a little practice, you might be a racing champ.

# SUPERSTARS OF THE MOUNTAINS

## As new as mountain biking is to the

world of sports, it already has stars. Men and women who have

been riding and winning races since the 1980s are now getting

into the Mountain Bike Hall of Fame.

Anyone who races mountain bikes knows who John

Tomac is. "Johnny T" has won more races than anyone else in

John Tomac is perhaps the most famous mountain-bike racer ever.

America's Alison Dunlap is a cross-country cycling champion.

the sport of mountain biking. He started out as a **BMX** racer, winning the nationals at age 16. Since then, Tomac has been the champion at cross-country uphill races, downhill, and time trials. Besides racing bikes, Tomac started his own mountain bike company called Tomac Bicycles. His company builds and sells bikes all over the world. Also, the company sponsors young riders and rising stars.

Another Hall of Famer is Ned Overend. Overend got his start racing motorbikes in high school. He took up mountain

Cross-country races can take riders through challenging trails.

biking in the 1980s and has dominated all types of racing since then. He has won six national titles and several World Cups over the years. But mountain biking is not the only sport at which Overend excels. He also races and wins **triathlons.** Like John Tomac, Overend gives a lot back to the sport of mountain biking. He is on the board of three groups that raise money to improve and build trails near Durango, Colorado, where he lives.

Perhaps the best-known female mountain biker is Juli Furtado. Like Tomac and Overend, Furtado started out in a different sport. When she was just 15, she became a member of the U.S. Ski Team. But after six years and six surgeries, she decided to give up skiing and start biking. Furtado didn't just ride; she won the U.S. National Series four times in a row and became the downhill world champion in 1992. She says of her sport, "People don't realize it, but the whole secret to mountain biking is pretty simple: the slower you go, the more likely it is you'll crash." Mountain biking sounds like a great sport for someone who used to race on skis.

Alison Sydor, from Canada, started mountain biking in 1991. She had been a road biker and loved to play ice hockey. During college at the University of Victoria, she decided to try a new sport: triathlons. She soon became the national junior

Mountain-bike racers can really move!

The adventure
never ends for the
mountain biker.

## MOUNTAIN BIKE HALL OF FAME

The Mountain Bike Hall of Fame and Museum, located in Crested Butte, Colorado, opened in 1988. The museum has gear and memories from the past 30 years of biking, along with antique bikes and parts. Press clippings, photos, and information about races are available for visitors to look at. More than 80 people who have made a contribution to the sport have been inducted into the Mountain Bike Hall of Fame. Next time you're in the neighborhood, park your bike and stop in for a visit. You can learn more about the Hall of Fame, its exhibits, and its members at *www.mtnbikehalloffame.com.*

champion at this sport. Then she began to specialize in mountain biking. Alison rose rapidly in the world of biking. She was the World Cup champion in 1996, 1998, and 1999. She also competed in two Olympics, winning a silver medal in the 1996 games in Atlanta, Georgia. Sydor says that 1996 was an interesting time to be a mountain biker. In earlier years, the sport had been ignored by many people. But then in Atlanta, it became an official Olympic event for the first time, and suddenly everyone wanted to be involved.

The Mountain Bike Hall of Fame will continue to fill up with riders such as these in the years to come. And the sport will continue to grow in popularity as more and more people see how much fun and adventure can be had with just a bike, a trail, and a helmet.

# GLOSSARY

**BMX**—Short for bicycle motocross. A race in which the bikes ride around a dirt track that has lots of bumps and banked curves.

**fat tires**—Tires measuring 26 inches (66 centimeters) in diameter and at least 2 inches (5 cm) wide, also called balloon tires.

**header**—Falling off the bike, head first, over the handlebars.

**klunkers**—The original mountain bikes, which were made from parts of many different bikes.

**off-road**—Having to do with places to ride that are not paved.

**shocks**—Devices attached to a bike's wheels that make riding easier and more comfortable by absorbing the bouncing on the trail.

**sprockets**—Toothed circles of metal around which bike chains move.

**toe-clips**—Cages that hold a rider's feet on the pedals.

**triathlons**—Races that involve a bike ride, a long run, and an ocean swim, one right after another.

# FIND OUT MORE

## On the Web

Visit our home page for lots of links about mountain biking:
*http://www.childsworld.com/links.html*

NOTE TO PARENTS, TEACHERS, AND LIBRARIANS: We routinely check our Web links to make sure they're safe, active sites—so encourage your readers to check them out!

## Books

Gibson, John, and J. P. Partland. *Mountain Bike Madness.* Osceola, Wis.: MBI Publishing, 2003.

Hughes, Morgan. *Juli Furtado: Rugged Racer.* Minneapolis: Lerner, 1998.

Immler, Robert. *Mountain Bicycling in the San Gabriels.* Berkeley, Calif.: Wilderness Press, 1987.

Jefferis, David. *All-Terrain Bikes.* Austin, Tex.: Raintree Steck-Vaughn, 2002.

King, Andy. *Play-by-Play Mountain Biking.* Minneapolis: LernerSports, 2001.

Weintraub, Aileen. *Mountain Biking.* Danbury, Conn.: Children's Press, 2003.

## Places to Visit

Mountain Bike Hall of Fame
331 Elk Avenue
Crested Butte, CO 81224
Telephone: 800-454-4505

# INDEX

## About the Author

Alicia and Rusty Schoenherr have been mountain biking all over the country since 1985. They live in Virginia with their three children, who bike everywhere! This is their first children's book.